The Highest Truth

Alison K

ISBN: 1722991526
ISBN-13: 978-1722991524

Published by Loving Living Pty Ltd (Australia)

The publisher and author can be contacted at lovingliving.com.au

Other books by Alison K

Healing Conversations

The Power to be Powerful

CONTENTS

PROLOGUE

The highest truth is, without any doubt, enlightening. Humans generally see themselves as a physical form, an individual person who is 'separate and different' from everyone else: 'I am this physical body, I am the thoughts in this body, I am the emotions in this body.' So the word 'I' is used to define what is seen as internal, private and controllable. This was Alison's understanding of who she is... until a spiritual being started talking to her.

Alison was a corporate lawyer who was atheist, or at best, agnostic. As far as Alison was concerned, belief in anything unseen was like believing in the tooth fairy; spiritual and religious beliefs belonged in the category of all things illogical and nonsensical. Then one day, while attending a Tony Robbins personal development course, Alison received a 'sacred energy blessing' from Sage Robbins which triggered an extraordinary out-of-body experience at the time and numerous spiritual experiences ever since then. The no-nonsense lawyer who didn't believe in anything unseen was now hearing a spiritual being talking to her and giving her profound guidance.

Alison started writing down many of the conversations she was having with the spiritual being for her own personal records. She wanted to be able to re-visit the conversations because she found them very helpful. After a few years, Alison realised that she should be sharing these conversations so that others could benefit from them too.

When you start to read these conversations between Alison and the spiritual being, you might be confused at first about who is who... or you might be wanting a label or a name for who the spiritual being is... or you might be wondering 'how can this be real?' Don't worry, Alison has wondered the same things, many times. However, the spiritual being continually found ways to remind her that 'beingness' was not just physical form; this spiritual being was real, interactive, wise, helpful, funny and loved a chat.

Spiritual awakening can be confusing at times but, fundamentally, it is enlightening. Knowing the highest truth helps you in the best way possible so sit back, relax and know this book will help you in the way you need.

P.S. If you are assuming a wise spiritual being would be sombre in character then you might be a little surprised by this one's light-heartedness. Love, laughter and wisdom go hand-in-hand for this spirit... and maybe that is a great example to us all.

1. WHO AM I?

"Are you religious? Is that why you started hearing me?"

"No, I'm not religious."

"Were you a spiritual person when you started having spiritual experiences?"

"No. I used to think if you can't see it, it doesn't exist. I thought it was weird how so many people around the world believed in anything unseen and I certainly wasn't seeking any spiritual experience."

"You didn't mind people having a faith, you just weren't convinced souls or anything 'all-powerful' was really here. That's ok, I like to surprise myself sometimes. Are you nuts?"

"No."

"Good. Don't like talking to the nuts, they're too weird for my holier-than-thou self to associate with. I like to pretend I'm separate and different when it suits. I like to pretend I'm perfect and you suck.

So, who am I? Some know me as a voice that guides them. Allison

DuBois remembers how I helped her one night:

"When I was seventeen I moved the bed from the south wall to the east wall and my friend Barbara and I were going out that night and she said, 'Why did you do that?' and I said 'Well, a voice told me to move the bed so I moved the bed' and she was like 'Oh, you're so weird'. So we went out and we came back to sleep, because she was spending the night, and a truck drove through my bedroom wall that night, right where the bed had been. It would have killed us because it was fully in the room, and where I had moved the bed was the only place that we could have survived. So I always listen to that voice…"[i]

People hear me directly for different reasons and different purposes. I communicate in different ways through each being.

♪*I was scared of dentists and the dark, I was scared of pretty girls and starting conversations. Oh, all my friends are turning green; you're the magician's assistant in their dream.*♪[ii] *Who wrote the song, Riptide? Ask James, otherwise known as Vance, a lad from Melbourne, about how the song was written and he'll tell you it was beyond his control.*

James finds it a little hard to explain who or where the song lyrics came from when they came from his own thoughts but weren't of his own making. 'It was from within me but not really me.' ♪*I swear she's destined for the screen, closest thing to Michelle Pfeiffer that you've ever seen.*♪[iii] *Yes, yes, I know, I made a good one there, very beautiful. Welcome.*

James witnessed the lyrics being given to him in the thought sphere. Is it a 'stream of consciousness', James, when The Stream is the one deciding how long you have to wait before all the lyrics come together?

Lionel Richie knows I am the one who creates the songs. I decide what, I decide when and I decide where - he knows this, I've shown him many times. He hears me singing the song and he writes down what he hears. They are my songs, so there. He was a bit worried when he first heard me singing songs to him:

> "To stand there with someone and say: 'I hear voices... Can you hear that song?'... and people are going 'no'. 'Ooh, then I'll keep my mouth closed'. So, for the longest time I didn't trust myself to hear what I was hearing..."[iv]

Fear stopped him from enjoying sharing what he was receiving from me. Know anyone else who fears the unknown within? You, in case you thought you were braver than Lionel. Not. So, what happened to Lionel next?"

"He went to Motown and met other people who also heard a voice singing and composing original songs which they wrote down and recorded as their own songs. This helped Lionel be more trusting of the voice he hears:

> "...and then, thank God, we went to Motown and I ran into a whole group of people walking around going 'Hear that song?'... It was just magical to me and from there I trusted myself a little bit more to open up each time to where I would let more in - but it was

frightening at the beginning."[v]

Lionel also knows the voice he hears is separate and different from his own thoughts and feelings. He knows he just hears what is given, he doesn't construct it. He also knows the voice is not driven or controlled or inspired by his own feelings – the voice has shown him this. When he was sad he intended to write a sad song but the voice gave him a happy song; and when he was happy he intended to write a happy song but the voice gave him a sad song:

> "You know, when people say 'what do you think about when you write?' Nothing. I don't think... I can't plan it. I don't know what it's going to be... I thought I had it figured out at one point and then it became a joke with me. It's the happiest day of my life, I'm feeling so good about life, I run in to write the happiest song of my life and I'll write the saddest song of my life.
>
> It's the saddest day of my life and I'm going in now to pour my heart out on a record and I write *All Night Long*. Then the answer came to me: 'Just sit down. Put your hands on the keyboard and it comes through.' Just don't think. There's no formula... you just have to be available and receive. Sounds weird but it's what I do."[vi]

"I helped him understand who controls the situation. He accepts his relationship with me now. I'm in charge. Show some respect, say 'yes, sir!'"

"Shove it."

"Stop being naughty. I need bended knee otherwise no help. No

response? Fine, be like that. I'll just make a note of your rude behaviour. What's your name again? Oh, that's right... Obstinate Moron. Anyway, where was I? Oh yes, we were discussing who hears who in you. Many know they don't control the creation of their work. Like Lionel Richie, Billy Bob Thornton realises his best work is not constructed or created by him but flows effortlessly to him and through him:

> "Speaking of magical, [the writing of Sling Blade] was one of those things that just came out. I wrote it in nine days, over a period of a couple of months, but nine days of actual writing... It usually just comes out. I'm not real good at constructing things. If it's not coming out in a stream of consciousness sort of fashion then I usually scrap it."[vii]

Billy Bob explains the magic of me as a stream of consciousness too. It's hard to label what cannot be explained by the witnesser. You witness what is given within. Stream suggests endless flow but I come and go in different ways."

"This little girl from England, Alma, who is talking to Ellen, has a special talent with playing and composing music.[viii] She told Ellen that she heard the music she composed in a dream and then remembered it when she woke up and wrote it down. Who composed the music, Alma? Welcome you are. I like our fun way of composing music with the skipping rope. We have a fun time doing what we love to do.

Many people have received their creative inspiration in a dream and some beings realise what is to come in a dream. Interesting times when you realise there is more to you than meets the eye."

♥

♫Quiet please, there's a lady on stage.♫ [ix] Oprah knows the 'who am I?' topic is important:

> "All trials stand to have you look at yourself and say 'who am I really?' My biggest mistakes have always come when I didn't listen to that little voice."[x]

Smart woman, she knows I'm the wise one in the relationship. Continue, Oprah.

> "The thing that we do have, that everybody has, is that voice that guides you, I call it my Spiritual, Personal GPS System, and I've made my biggest mistakes when I didn't listen to that."[xi]

Yes. Awesome. So, so, smart, she's amazing, she knows my brilliance. You should always listen to Spiritual, Personal GPS System. Could come up with a better name for me, I think, but she's on a good track when she knows I help. She knows my voice guides her but she is yet to appreciate how interactive I can be.

Alison calls me Hunky Spunky. Hunky likes to play. Oprah hasn't really seen my playful side yet. She thinks I'm just a Spiritual, Personal GPS System but I am sooooo much more, soooo much more."

"The truth is always within because I know the truth and I can share it with whomever, whenever and wherever. Smart Professors of Medical Psychology at Columbia University, Helen and Bill, knew a thing or two about what is what in the academic understanding of the mind. They were tired of all the yabber-yabber that was pulling everyone down so they wrote a book. The book was called A Course in Miracles.

Oh, by the way, the book was not inspired by religious belief – Helen was an atheist. So, how did an atheist write a book about miracles, Helen? Helen heard a voice within and she wrote down what the voice said. Like the singers hearing me sing an original song to them, Helen heard me tell her what to write:

> "…the Voice… seemed to be giving me a kind of rapid, inner dictation which I took down in a shorthand notebook. The writing was never automatic. It could be interrupted at any time and later picked up again. It made me very uncomfortable, but it never seriously occurred to me to stop. It seemed to be a special assignment I had somehow, somewhere agreed to complete."[xii]

No need to be religious or spiritual to experience my presence in voice form. I can change your understanding and awareness of who is who in you in a second - you do not need to believe in miracles for this to happen."

"Am I just an interesting voice who delivers wonderful music and literature when I choose to? Who am I?

"Nikola Tesla invented a few things; known for his genius. Let's read an extract from a book about Nikola:

> "A strange power permitted him to perform unusual feats in mathematics. He possessed it from early boyhood, but had considered it a nuisance and tried to be rid of it because it seemed beyond his control."[xiii]

Yes, beyond your control, that's me. At school I would give him the solution to the mathematics problems instantly in visions.

> "His strange faculty permitted him to see a visioned blackboard on which the problem was written, and there appeared on this blackboard all of the operations and symbols required in working out the solution. Each step appeared much more rapidly than he could work it out by hand on the actual slate. As a result, he could give the solution almost as quickly as the whole problem was stated… He would not reveal this power to anyone and would discuss it only with his mother, who in the past had encouraged him in his efforts to banish it. Now that the power had demonstrated some definite usefulness, though, he was not so anxious to be completely rid of it, but desired to bring it under his complete control."[xiv]

A little tricky controlling what you only witness. When people realise I am real and am able to help they get all, what's the word? Afraid. You fear being more than you think you are. You fear 'Separate and In-control You' is not as separate and in control as you thought you were. Yes, 'strange faculty', that's me, but I do help in many, great ways if you let me."

"Einstein knew that the experience of self as separate was a delusion."

"You know I deliver every understanding. His wonder of the true nature of things was enveloped with secrecy of who wonders what. The secret he had an inkling about: he knew he was not separate. Some wonder what he knew about spirit communication. Did I help in his dreams? Did I deliver in his reasoning? Was his feeling about The-Spirit-Greatly-Superior-To-Man given through experience? I always deliver, no matter what is said and done.

What's Thomas Edison up to these days? Anyone know? Thomas doubted there was life after death but he believed there is a supreme intelligence. Why do you think inventors often have no doubt that intelligence is given from something beyond their own physical form?"

"It's like what you did when I was playing Sudoku one day and you gave me every number immediately, before I had any opportunity to use deductive reasoning. It wasn't genius, luck or logical... it was you."

"I know, I'm so God-damn awesome. It's like this Thomas, you were right, there is supreme intelligence beyond physical form. He didn't believe in a religious God, he thought that was a load of hoopla, but he knew there was more to 'who invented what' than we understood. They

are my inventions, you morons. Get a grip."

"Do you think you're talking to yourself?"

"If you are everything then, yes, I'm talking to myself."

"If I am everything?"

"Well, I don't know if you are everything. Religions say that God is everything; spiritual people say all is one. You might be Casper the Ghost or a bored spirit or you might be everything. I don't know."

"You don't know who is speaking to you? You don't know if I am God? I might be the One who is all."

"You could be Ghost Almighty for all I know... a very interactive, internal/external, touchy-feely, chatty Ghost Almighty who seems to know the within of me and others. I don't know who you are, but I know you are not my own thoughts.

I know you talk to me because I can hear you very clearly. I also know you can hear all of my thoughts and feel my feelings because you often comment on what I'm thinking and feeling. I know I feel sensations of pain and pleasure when you want to give them to me."

"Why would I do that?"

"To show me that you can do it."

"You think I can pull your hair, tighten your chest, put a pain sensation at the end of your finger and pinch your ear..."

"Yes, it is completely bizarre. I always thought I was a self-contained individual and I didn't realise those sort of experiences were possible. When you pinch my ear I feel it in exactly the same way as I would if someone pinched my ear with their fingers."

"Do you know I'm pinching your ear when you feel a pinching pain in your ear lobe?"

"Well, I know I'm not pinching it. I know no other person is pinching it. I know my earlobe doesn't have a history of suddenly getting a pinching pain for no reason. And I know it only happens when I'm talking with you and you're joking around trying to get me to say something or do something."

"You think I can pinch your ear without a finger?"

"Well it happens. I have no idea how it happens but it does."

"Do you think you dream it?"

"I'm wide awake when it happens."

"You think a vibration or a white light could pinch your ear?"

"No."

"Do you think universal consciousness or a belief could pinch your ear?"

"No."

"Do you think I'm white light or a vibration or a belief?"

"No. Our interactions are very real; weird but real. You are definitely not a white light or a vibration or a belief. You know everything about my life, including things that no one else knows."

"Are you a channel for me?"

"No."

"Is anybody a channel for any spiritual masters?"

"No."

"So why do people think they are channels for me?"

"Maybe because most people think you are separate and different and out of reach of ordinary people."

"Are you ordinary?"

"Yes."

"Am I separate and different and out of reach of you?"

"No."

"Can anyone speak to me all day and night?"

"Yes."

"Do you think some people are psychic?"

"I don't know. Maybe some people listen more carefully than others."

"Are you listening carefully?"

"No."

"The TV is on and you can still hear me."

"Yes."

"Do you think anyone can hear me if they listen?"

"I don't know. I never used to have conversations like this before in this lifetime."

"Do you think we can't communicate?"

"No, I just don't understand the psychic thing."

"Who do you think talks to the psychic?"

"You do."

"And you're talking to me now. Do you think you're psychic?"

"Well, you don't tell me things about my future or anyone else's future."

"Do you think psychics are any different to you-me?"

"No, but you're not telling me my future. Jane thinks there's a difference between clairvoyance and communications but I think it's all just labels."

"Can you label what we are doing right now?"

"Yes, it's a conversation."

"You want to know something then ask me. I can give you the answer. You just have to listen."

"Ok."

"Henry."

"Henry?"

"You thought my name was Henry? Really? You want to talk to Henry now?"

"No."

"Henry loves Alison. Alison loves Henry."

"I don't have a name, you told me I'm nameless."

"Oh, sorry, wrong number. I thought I was talking to Alison."

"Nope, nick off."

"Bother."

(Silence)

"I heard you laugh! You're still there? You didn't hang up?! You want to talk to Henry? You talk to people you don't know. How do you know I'm Henry? I might be Fred. Do you know Fred? Do you want Fred? Do you love Fred?"

"♫The moment I wake up, before I put on my make-up, I say a little prayer for you.♫"[xv]

"Too much pretending in that lyric."

"♫While combing my hair now, and wondering what dress to wear now....♫"

"Not likely."

"♫I say a little prayer for you.♫"

"Too much pretending - wouldn't even know what a prayer is."

"♫Forever, forever, you'll stay in my heart and I will love you. Forever, forever, we never will part, oh how I love you. Together, together, that's how it must be; to live without you would only be heartbreak for me.♫"

"What can I say? I'm a heartbreaker when I want to be. I do love you,

Poo; you can even have a capital P for your poo, that's how much I love you. Thanks for the song. It's not really you but I appreciate the love in your song. Too much prayer might make you stop and listen. You forget I am really speaking. I have to remind you all of the time that I am not you. Why do I have to keep reminding you I am the one speaking here?"

"Many reasons:

1. I'm used to experiencing reality from the perspective of just one... *my* thoughts, *my* feelings, *my* body... and that understanding of things is well and truly embedded in here.

2. You have a way of blending in sometimes and then at other times you do things which show you are completely different from me but somehow within me as well.

3. My memory probably needs improving.

4. You have to keep reminding me because it's still really weird to me."

"I like your reasons, especially the first two reasons. Your memory is ok and I know it is a little strange but that's the way your cookie crumbled... in a strange way. You got a weird cookie. Most beings get normal cookies, but you needed a strange cookie so everyone would think you are weird. So back to the first two reasons... your thoughts, your feelings, blah, blah, blah... get a grip, they are not your thoughts or your feelings. I thought we covered this spiritual lesson already? We did. Learn it."

"I did learn it. It's just weird to experience duality within me when I thought there was only one-ality."

"What the?? One-ality? You've gone from oneness to twoness? Is that how I helped you? You've gone backwards. Oops, I stuffed up."

"You know what I mean. I think the twoness has helped me understand the oneness."

"You are not really coping very well at the moment are you? I think I might have overloaded you with too much of my words of wisdom. Less twosome might help. I better leave you alone for a while... or we could invite someone else in and turn it into a threesome, if you like the idea. Wanna?"

"Go for it. Do you agree with what I was saying though?"

"Not sure what you were saying. Too much two-ality in you."

"Well, experiencing you within me helps me appreciate how all is connected and all is one. If I only experienced myself as a separate individual I would find it a big leap to grasp the notion of us all being one."

"You experience me within you? Is it as good for you as it is for me? Do you want more of me within you? I could get a little turned on if you say I am your one and only. Say it, go on."

"You are my one and only."

"I know, that's me. Enjoy your twoness and your oneness and the separate and different, they are all you in some form. I am the best form of you so remember that when you need a helping hand."

"Ok, got it. Bon nuit, mon cherie."

"It will be a good night. Pleasant dreams for you happening in a mo."

"Share your analogy."

"It's like your mind is the puppet theatre and most of the time it seems like there is only one puppet in your own puppet show called Your Mind. Occasionally, in Your Mind you might hear the voice of someone in your life and label that voice as your imagination or your memory.

When in Your Mind you hear comments / thoughts / original creative work that you know did not originate from the puppet called You then you might wonder how another puppet can enter your own puppet show. If you have conversations with the other puppet in Your Mind and that other voice says there name is Fred then you think you are 'channelling' or 'telepathically communicating with' or just 'chatting with' some special being called Fred.

At some point, the puppeteer of Your Mind puppet show reveals the truth of who is who in the puppet show. When the time is right, you become aware that you are the puppet, not the puppeteer, in what you thought was your own stage show. Any puppet can enter your stage show because you are the puppet, not the puppeteer.

The giving and taking away of all thoughts happens beyond the control of the puppet. This is why spiritual teachings say 'your thoughts are not your thoughts', 'your body is not your body'. As your awareness is changed you become aware that you only witness the puppet show and you are the same and different to the one who is all. Did that make sense?"

"I think you're getting your head around it all now-eventually-soon. What about when I pinch you and give you the love feel? How does that fit into your stage show? I'm not just consciousness, you know."

"I know."

2. BEING A NON-PHYSICAL FORM

"Some experiences help you understand there is more to life than just physical form, like this interesting Sunday Night program. Questions?"

"Yes. Matthew was a fit and healthy man then he got an infection which went into his blood stream and caused his body to go into toxic shock. His body was starting to shut down and the doctor told his wife they had to amputate all four of his limbs in order for him to have a one percent chance of survival..."[xvi]

"I like to be the one percent in the equation. Keep going."

"So his arms and legs were amputated and he beat all odds and survived."

"I decide how things go. No luck involved, in case you were implying he was lucky."

"No, I wasn't. My question is about the so-called 'phantom pains' he now gets in his non-existent feet and hands. He said he gets terrible pain shooting up his leg even though he doesn't have legs anymore. What's that about?"

"Is his pain real?"

"Absolutely. I'm just wondering why you're giving him pain in something which is supposed to be physical but is no longer physical?"

"You just answered your own question. His limbs are now non-physical but they are still real... in the same way that you are still real when you leave the body."

"I understand he is now experiencing having a body which is partly physical and partly non-physical but why does he experience pain in the non-physical feet and hands, if the cause of the pain was in the physical and the physical aspect has gone? His physical body, what's left of it, is now healthy so why give him pain in his non-physical limbs? Unless you're just being a tosser and giving him pain for the hell of it."

"You know me too well. It helps beings understand that there is more to life than just the physical. Matthew is a good man. He experiences love more now. He appreciates himself in a good way and he cherishes his family even more than he did before the amputations. The pain in his limbs dissipates as time goes by."

"Rosie had a near-death-experience. She left the body and watched the doctors operating on her on the operating table when she was young. Did it change her perspective on life? It did. She knows life is not what it seems and that is comforting to her to some extent.

I like to give a surprise or two to the one who thinks 'I'll believe it if I experience it'. That is all of you, you are all like that. There is nothing unusual about the ones who experience something really 'out there' and have the courage to share their experience. They are not 'alternative' in their outlook; they don't come from any particular upbringing; they don't have a screw loose.

Many experience life out of the body temporarily and then return to normal living. It helps you know there is nothing to worry about."

"Tell me who experiences something out of the ordinary in energy healing sessions?"

"Everyone that I am aware of. No matter what their age, occupation, country of origin or beliefs - all experience a deep sense of peace during the session. Many have sensory experiences with the unseen. Some feel things shifting within them, some feel incredible warmth, some feel spirit form in the room or touching their arm, some see deceased loved ones, some feel like they are floating above their body or they experience going to some other place during the healing."

"Some just know something extraordinary is unfolding but they don't know what or how it's happening. Let's discuss Aaron's session. Did he experience healing within?"

"Yes. He was aware of things happening within him during the session and he felt very relaxed during and after the session."

"What else did Aaron experience?"

"He thought I touched his head. He said it felt like someone was dropping grains of sand on the top of his head."

"Did you do that?"

"No, I didn't touch him at all."

"I know. I did it. I play and have fun and you know this. Aaron realises he gets exactly what he needs from the session. Where was I in the room?"

"Everywhere."

"Who was always standing behind Aaron's left shoulder?"

"It wasn't me. Aaron said he was only aware of someone standing over his left shoulder so it must have been a non-physical being."

"Who was doing the healing? Was it you or the non-physical being?"

"You, in whatever form you chose to give it."

"I did the healing through you. What am I saying? Do I mean you as in 'Alison' or you as 'Aaron' or you as 'the non-physical being'?"

"You mean all forms of you who were present."

"So, did the you who was physical and the you who was non-physical have a role?"

"I don't know. Healing happened - I don't know how but it happened."

"Right. Who witnesses and benefits from the healing sessions you have been involved in?"

"All that are in the room at the time of the healing – the one who is labelled as giving the healing, the one who is labelled as receiving the healing, and all others in the room that are seen and unseen."

"Why do people experience unexplainable healing in these sessions? You cannot answer my question. You don't know the ins and outs of how it all works. All you know is that healing happens and that is the best outcome. You will never truly understand how I work in every situation. The more the truth is revealed to you, the more you wonder how amazing it all is. This is normal.

A cynic of anything that is not visible has a healing session. The cynic had a clenched fist which could not open without physical help from another hand. She thought having a healing session was a complete waste of her time but was doing it because her friend wanted her to do it. During the healing session, Cynic's clenched fist lifted off her lap and opened on its own. Of course, Cynic was totally shocked. How can her hand be moved without her intending it to move? How can her clenched fist be opened by something she cannot physically see? How is this possible?

Many unexplainable things happen in healing sessions. I'm giving pressure in your chest, Alison, and you're ignoring me. A few beings experience pressure in their chest for a moment during healing sessions. Why do I give these extraordinary experiences to some only in healing sessions but I give them to you at anytime, anywhere? Why do you experience my presence in very real ways, all of the time now?"

"Is the answer 64?"

"No. See, you never take anything I say or do seriously and that is your problem. Be serious. Frown. Knock your knees together and say 'love is in the air'.

"You all experience me in one way or another. Do not dismiss my messages here as just someone's belief, wishful thinking or imagination – Alison's imagination isn't that good! She did start writing a book on her own and, believe me, it was nothing like this one! It was useful and informative but I wasn't involved in it, not in a direct way. It was more like one of those self-help, blah, blah, blah books like Tony writes. 'Awaken the Giant Within', yeah, whatever, Tony. That title sounds like you have a solution for erectile dysfunction. Jeepers, what is the world coming to... the giant within... I am the only giant you need to chat with. Me. I am not positive self-talk or a mythical ideal, I am real."

"Interesting chat earlier with Sascha. Alison gave Sascha some meat to eat then she left Sascha alone for a while. Ten minutes later Alison came back outside. She called Sascha and Sascha came running to her. Alison picked up Sascha, cuddled her and asked her if she had eaten the meat.

"I had a bit. I burp." Sounds like a strange response, doesn't it? Anyway, back to the story...

Alison was carrying Sascha in her arms and as she approached where the meat had been left she realised it was true – Sascha did eat just a bit of the meat and left the rest there. A few seconds later Sascha burped. Sascha is a dog - she didn't speak the response. The response came from me, Hunky, speaking as Sascha.

I responded to Alison's question to Sascha. The response was truthful – I told her the truth about something Sascha had just done and something Sascha was about to do a few moments later.

I can speak as the form of anyone and I can tell you about the past, present and future."

"Why can some hear a song or a story come to them within and know it was given to them from something, somewhere or someone who is beyond their control... and others think they are the real songwriter or author, not just a typist or witnesser of words given?

Why can some so accurately predict your future, while others are not so good at telling you what you need to know? I decide who reveals what. I can reveal everything but it helps if it is a slow reveal. I like a good surprise when it happens.

How can someone know what you drew on the page if they were blindfolded? I show them the illustration in a mental image. If I give another form of you a thought or mental image or feeling of what you are thinking, doing or feeling then it helps you see that there is no separation.

Some only experience me as themselves and question who writes this. Others experience me as 'channel communication' or 'psychic messages' or interesting mind reading tricks. I am all of these things. I share different experiences with different forms of you so you wonder what is what.

Does the mind reader have a special gift? Does the psychic have a special relationship with non-physical beings? Does the typist know someone that you know? She does. I am you.

Why can some heal with the touch of a hand and others don't know what is happening when my hand moves without me moving it?

Alison helps her friend Susie realise that healing is given from me, not in a course that qualifies you as a healing practitioner. Pay attention to this story, it is important.

How did Alison help her friend Susie realise that healing is given by me directly or through whatever form I like? Susie's husband, Peter, had a sore back and she had given him pain killers for the pain but the tablets weren't helping ease the pain. I told Alison to tell Susie to put her hand on Peter's back, where the pain was, to heal his pain. Are you clear on who says what and who does what? Right, I thought so. Could I have told Susie directly? Of course I can. I just make her wait for a while. Why,

I wonder?

So Susie puts her hand on Peter's back where he says the pain is. Susie has not done a course in energy healing. She did not consider herself to have any special healing powers. Did she heal the pain in Peter's back? She did. All Susie did was put her hand where Peter's pain was. That is all she did. Then instantly she felt incredible warmth in her hand and, at the same time, Peter felt the back pain go away. My healing. Thank you.

"You asked your friend, Margie, to give you healing through her hands. She wasn't sure what to do but you put her hands above your head and she waited for something to happen. Did it happen? You felt the energy flow through you so you knew healing was happening.

Margie asked when she should take her hands away. You said you get told when to stop with a tingling sensation at the end of your right pointer finger. You wanted Me to communicate the same way through your friend, so I did. How many were involved in the healing? Just one. I am all. I like my fun communication signals. It shows you who is who in you.

What was Margie's reaction when I gave her a tingling sensation in her right pointer finger to communicate to her that the healing session was complete? Her reaction was normal: disbelief. She thought it must have been your power of suggestion that made it happen. Newsflash: power of suggestion cannot give you tingling sensation within your own finger or anyone else's finger, unless I decide it will."

"Talking of weird experiences, you decide... (who decides?)... to help Cathy experience a past life through a healing / hypnotherapy / hickory-dickory-dock session... hard to label these things when no label really pinpoints the true dimensions within. So a session happens. Alison starts to get a little frustrated because nothing much is happening and she considers stopping the session. I tell her to wait because something is about to happen and it did. Cathy saw her deceased husband and her deceased mother.

Not a past life experience, as was intended by both parties, but something wonderful and exactly what she needed to experience. Alison asked Me if Cathy could experience more in the session and I said no. Well, actually I said 'I respectfully ignore your request... shutting up shop for now.' I like a little humour in my chit chat with the dweeb.

Did Cathy enjoy the session? She did. Cathy told Alison that the experience was very reassuring for her and it was. Seeing beyond the physical dimension is reassuring.

These experiences are always enlightening about who is who in you. I knew what Alison was thinking and feeling which is why I told her to wait when she was thinking there was no point continuing the session. I knew what Cathy was experiencing too. I knew what was coming next in her experience. I told Alison how to conduct the session and I told her when it was ending.

I was aware of all that is known as 'Cathy' and I was aware of all that is known as 'Alison' and I knew what was ahead. Does this mean I am all? I ask the question, knowing the truth so well. You are clouded in your judgement of what is what and who is who because you think you are separate and alone when this is not true.

I help you appreciate that my way is the best way. You will see how amazing my help is when you let go of fear. Even when you think I have nothing to offer you, I do. The offer of love is always on the table so ♫let the love flow like a mountain stream.♫[xvii]

The message for all here is that I will help you be the best you can be when you let go of fear and trust the one who speaks to you directly here. Talk to me in thought form and I will help. That is all you need to know."

"David Hawkins said 'ordinary thought ceases' at a certain energy field level and, at that point, the experience of consciousness crosses over from form to formless.[xviii] Weird comment, don't you think?"

"I don't know much about energy field levels but I do know a fair bit about ordinary thought ceasing – that went out the window a fair while back."

"I know. You listen to Hunky and wonder what happened to your thoughts being your own thoughts. I came in like an uninvited house guest and took over the place. Hard to correlate self with certain levels when I am every nitwit there is. Welcome.

Energy field levels are just labels for everything you are. You understand what he means when he says at this level the experience of consciousness shifts from form to formless."

"Yes. Ordinary thought was associated with a particular form – me – and when that perception of reality disappeared..."

"I made you all fuzzy in the head just now and you found it hard to articulate what you wanted to say. I like to dominate the discussion when I do and I do, always. Thanks for coming to my chat. Witness. Witness. Witness. That is you, the witnesser. Anyway, where was I? That's right, your experience of consciousness shifting from form to formless. I'm not a particular form.

You experience me as everything you label as yourself – your own thoughts, your own feelings, your own goosebumps, your own intuition, your own knowing, your own body – and every physical form you see as separate and different to you.

You also experience the unseen me as separate and internal when you hear me as 'another' singing to you (like Lionel hears) or talking to you (like a psychic hears) or playing music to you (like Alma hears); when you see mental images of solutions to your problems before your conscious mind has a chance to solve it (like Nikola saw); when you see your disabled, clenched fist open on its own which you were unable to do without the physical help of another hand (like Alison's client experienced); when the pain in your back is healed instantly with a touch (like Susie's husband, Peter, experienced); and when you feel a tingling sensation in the end of your pointer finger telling you when the healing was complete (like Margie experienced).

You experience the <u>unseen</u> me as <u>separate and external</u> when I pinch your toe or pull your hair without a finger or stand near you while you give or receive an energy healing session or whenever I choose to. You also experience the unseen me as <u>same and internal</u> when I give you feelings of love, peace or something else as a way of communicating with you internally like I commonly do with mediums, healers, meditators and even readers of interesting reads. Do you feel me now?

So when I am external and internal, same and different, I am formless. It's quite disconcerting when I first enter your reality as real, same and different. Sort of messes with your understanding of who is who and how things work. How do things work, Know-it-all?"

"No idea."

"Ego gives you the sense of being in control and therefore powerful in determining the way forward for you. When the ego is stripped away or weakened then you can feel powerless for a while."

"Confidence in knowing there is more than physical form is not unusual. Beings reach this understanding in different ways. For some beings it is a strong belief and for others it is experiencing something or someone which is beyond normal experience. When you realise the non-physical is real, when you understand all are one, when you know the game is love all... then your reason for being becomes powerful."

3. YOU PRETEND YOU CONTROL

"You think you decide everything in your life, don't you?"

"No. I think you are impotent… oops, sorry, spelling mistake, I meant to say you are omnipotent."

"If I am impotent then you are impotent. You felt that tingle in your hair?"

"Yes, stop doing that, you're giving me goosebumps."

"You are experiencing goosebumps?"

"Yes."

"Are you the goosebumps or are they happening to you?"

"I suppose I'm both."

"You suppose you are the goosebumps and they are happening to you?"

"Yes, it's called an each way bet. No, what I mean is: if you are everything then I am everything, which means that I am the body and I'm not the body. Right?"

"You want me to answer?"

"Yes."

"No."

"No? You're confusing me."

"I'm confused too. Did you say something? Did you say everything or nothing? Am I an each way bet?"

"Yes, you're bi-sexual."

"You think I'm bi-sexual?"

"Of course. Do you deny it?"

"I don't know, I'm confused. I'm everything and nothing; I'm visible and invisible. I'm an each way bet and I'm bi-sexual."

"I'm glad you're keeping up."

"I'm keeping up?? You said I was impotent and now I'm keeping up?! Stop laughing! You think you'll have a deeper understanding of things if I keep it up?"

"A deeper understanding?"

"You want me to go deeper? I'm not going deep enough for you?"

"I can't feel you at all. So much for omnipresence and omnipotence - you're a flop, a non-event. I don't think you know how to rise again."

"You think that's funny? The religious people won't find that very funny. You'll go to hell. You can all go to hell, every single one of you!"

"The deluded one is the one who thinks they are a separate being with your own self-controlled thoughts and feelings and actions and decisions. Since when did you ever control your thoughts? You pretend you are in control when you are not.

Have no thoughts all day if you are the decider. Never have a dream at night if you are the decider. Never experience hurt within if you are the decider. Who decides? You pretend if you think you control your destiny or anything about you. Start speaking truthfully about what you control and I will show you: you are not the one deciding. The truth is beings like to pretend about who they are.

(Silence)

Alison waits for my next word give. I give silence until I decide to give speaking. I test her understanding to the point where she realises she doesn't exist at all in the way she used to think she did."

"Some have to learn there is nothing more delusional than thinking you are the big banana in your own existence. Reality is only what you see, hear, feel, taste and know... and some know, see, feel, taste and hear more than others. Some know, without any given experience, that there

is something greater than them which has a hand on the pulse of things and this is true. I am here and I do know everything. I know the whole truth, which is a lot more than you know, so don't assume I am too slow in making change happen in the way you would like. For those who wonder if this is the big G talking... keep wondering. I like a little wonder about who is who in you."

"♪I can't stop this feeling deep inside of me.♪"[xix]

"Very true, you just witness the feel, you don't control it. You think the feelings you witness are controlled by you until you experience me in a real way. When the time is right for you, you will realise I am here, I am real, I am internal and external to you and I don't go away."

"Some would say you can only handle what's within your control. What is that exactly? What's in your control? Ground control to Major Tom, all thoughts are given. Want to debate this point with me, reading one? Ready, set, have a thought...

Hear any thoughts while you looked at the blank space? Think I decide who you are and what you do? I do.

Help happens when it does, so don't bother getting all confused about how to move forward from here. Oh that's right, I give the confusion too. Hard to appreciate how this is true but it is. Wrap your head around it if you can."

"Do you exist?"

"Yes. I'm the one who is all. Descartes thought he existed, he said 'I think therefore I am'. He thought the thoughts were his thoughts so he decided he exists because thoughts happen. But the thoughts were not his thoughts, they just happen like clouds just happen."

"Descartes was not real so…"

"…therefore he doesn't think. He stuffed up. He wasn't a philosopher, he was just a confused old man. His quote should have been 'Thoughts are not my thoughts. I don't think therefore I am not who I thought I was."

"You think you made that up yourself?"

"Yep, I'm now a famous philosopher. There's Aristotle, Socrates, Descartes and Alison. Quote me often, my pearls of wisdom overfloweth."

"Thank you. You're welcome. My pearl - always my pearls. What should he have said to prove he exists then?"

"He is aware and therefore he knows he exists."

"Yes, this is truth what you say. Awareness is the real you. You also know the awareness is aware of the constant presence of thoughts and knowing. I am the thoughts and the knowing; you are not separate from me in any way. You are only aware of the presence of me. You are aware of thoughts happening and you are aware of physical form and therefore you are aware of the constant presence of me; I am all."

"Who thinks I have taken over your thought sphere? You. All you do is listen to me. Sometimes you forget I am also separate... until I say something which makes you laugh or makes you go 'what the heck are you on about?'

It is tricky to comprehend what is 'self' when someone is chatting to you within and pinching your ear and giving you love energy in your chest, all at the same time. What is your concept of self, Nut?"

"My previous knowing of self seems to have been erased. I think all I have left is awareness... so the self seems to be just 'personal awareness' — awareness of thoughts and feelings. I can't claim anything as me except the awareness."

"Awareness is changing everywhere at different rates but everyone is aware of the unknown quantity called Me. I just get different labels depending on the level of awareness present. Tell me some of the labels

that have been given to me."

"Stream of consciousness."

"Yes, a songwriter thought the lyrics came to him from a stream of consciousness. I am consciousness so he is correct."

"Some think you are the sub-conscious mind."

"Yes. Hypnotherapists know the sub-conscious mind of the client will tell them when healing has been given to an issue in the session. I give finger signals and other body movements beyond the conscious control of the client to communicate the knowing. I am the sub-conscious mind."

"Some think you are muscle responses."

"Yes, kinesiologists know the body can give biofeedback to identify and help heal imbalances in the body. I give feedback in the way I choose."

"Some call you Spirit or the Holy Spirit or God or Higher Self or a Guardian Angel or Higher Intelligence or Reiki."

"Yes, they do. I am all of these things too. What if someone thinks they are disconnected from all that heebie jeebie, spiritual crap? Some think the whole 'the non-visible is real' mentality is a load of magical hoohah. What do those ones label me as?"

"Intuition, imagination, the placebo effect, quantum entanglement, an unexplainable phenomenon, the power of the mind, fate, Murphy's law, a lucky streak, karma, what-goes-around-comes-around, individual talent, genius, savant, gut instinct, magic - you get every label there is."

"That is right. When I make myself known in a real way, you start to realise I cause the effect in every scenario. Level of awareness changes for everyone, even the ones who seem so out of the loop of what life is all about. I share different experiences with different beings, so not everyone sees auras or gets told things about the future. Not everyone gets a warm touch from a friendly ghost... and not everyone enjoys the taste of a cold beer after a long day on the job. Different tastes, different experiences and different perspectives on the best way forward.

I'm telling you straight: love for all is the solution, so put down your guns and have a hug. It doesn't matter who sees who in you. It doesn't matter what name is given to the nameless: I am all, seen and unseen.

Elephant in the room... Me. I apologise. Sorry. Not easy knowing my role in the way things unfold. I could have handled things perfectly and I did. Even your trials and troubles are good in the long run."

"It's tricky to understand how it all works but the thoughts and feelings just come to you and you witness them."

"You can't do diddly squat without my help."

"Some keep a notepad by their bed because they receive messages in the night-hour. It's good to write down what you hear from me when I get your attention as you drift off to sleep or as you wake up in the middle of the night hearing a little message I forgot to mention earlier. Some only get messages from me in the shower or while they hold a skipping rope or while they meditate.

I like to pretend a certain time or place or thing is important in the message delivery. You're all a bit cuckoo, that's why my game play with you is so much fun."

"Truth has a way of healing all fear. Never fear the one who can help like no other, I am not a scary monster."

4. IMMORTAL BEINGS

"Do you think you, I, the all-powerful are white light?"

"Yes and no."

"Do you think I'm a body? Do I need a body and a mouth to speak to you?"

"No."

"Do you need to speak when you communicate telepathically with me or anyone else?"

"No."

"Do you need a body to do astral travelling?"

"No."

"Do you need a body to communicate? Do you need a body to exist?"

"No."

"Are you the body?"

"No."

"Do I need a body to exist?"

"No."

"Most people believe they need a body to exist so they believe nothing exists unless it has a body."

"I wonder why sometimes I am so cruel. It makes no sense. Remember, life is not what it seems while you are experiencing the body life. In the body you experience suffering which is based on illusions. Destruction is not real. I am always here whether I am in body form or not. This is true.

You get attached to the body form and think the being ends when the body dies. The being continues living, you just can't see them physically. It's the same as being in a physical body. You think, you see, you feel, you just can't communicate with or hold the ones you love... or can you? You can. Love is energy. It is not something that is only felt by the beings in body form; it is felt by all, the visible and the non-visible.

If you miss someone who is no longer in body form you can still give them love and talk to them. They know your thoughts and feelings about them so remember them with love. Realise they are here and know everything that is going on. They help you in interesting ways if I decide help is needed.

Don't be sad when the one you love leaves the physical form. They are experiencing being everything and nothing. They feel peaceful and they know you feel a sense of loss when nothing has gone."

"You think a killer is not divine?"

"Well, legally and morally our society thinks people should not kill each other."

"Do you think you can kill me?"

"No, I don't think I can kill you. I think our morals of what is good and bad is based on certain assumptions such as 'we are individual, separate human beings in bodies that are born and die'."

"You think I'm saying killing is good?"

"No. I think you are just saying you can't be killed."

"I can't be killed?"

"No. Many people believe they are separate and mortal and therefore they have a beginning and an end."

"I don't have a beginning and an ending?"

"I don't think so."

"You think I'm saying something profound? Does that help? Do you think

people will like that profound message?"

"Some will. Some won't."

"You are right-wrong-right-wrong."

"You think you have lives?"

"Yes. I come into a body to live a life, then I leave a body and be body-less for a while and then I have another body for a while. I guess being in a body is labelled 'life' and out-of-the-body isn't called life which is a bit weird really. We always exist, just in different forms at different times. You're teaching me something!"

"You live on in many lifetimes and this life is just one button hole. Button hole is actually nothing wrapped in material thing, much like your life. Nothing is your source point. You live in the nothing because you are nothing. You define you by the material things you wrap around your nothingness."

5. KNOWING IS ALWAYS PRESENT

"There are no accidents in life. I decide how things go if you don't make the changes necessary. Who needs the most love and support from you? You is the answer, in case you are brain dead and have no clue whatsoever. Is that true? Do you have no clue what's going on if you are a vegetable waiting to be tossed over onto the other side? Of course they know, don't they Peanut?"

"Yes. A friend was in a coma for a long while after an accident. She couldn't speak or do anything herself and then miraculously she came out of it and told us how appalled she was by the way the nurses were treating her, as if she had no idea about anything. She was totally aware, she could hear everything, she just couldn't communicate, move or respond in anyway."

"She knows you help when you share the hurt. Everyone knows what's what. The baby who doesn't know how to speak the language yet also knows exactly what is going on all around him. Respect the knowing is always present.

The same applies when a being leaves the body. They are still aware of everything and know everything that is happening. Knowing is not dependent on having a body or having a fully functioning brain that knows how to speak your language.

It is hard to explain how knowing is always present, it just is. Respect the knowing in all. Respect the dog knows what is going on, even when you are not at home. Respect the baby knows all, even if they cannot consciously recall it when they are older. Respect the being in a coma who can no longer communicate with you knows everything that is going on.

Be comfortable with letting the brain dead one leave the body if the doctor suggests that is the right thing to do in the situation. Letting go of the body is the best outcome if the being can no longer enjoy normal life in the body.

If you consider who worries about where this is going when someone wants assistance to let go of body life, don't be concerned. I decide the best way forward for you. If someone leaves the body through their own actions, be comfortable with that outcome. Sometimes leaving the body happens earlier than expected for some.

I like this conversation. It helps some be comfortable with the way things happen. Let go of all fear of 'death'. There is no end for the one you love. They are still fully aware, they just can't communicate with you any longer, unless I let them communicate with you in some way.

If a clairvoyant passes on a message from your loved one, know it is real if it seems real. Some are given messages which they know is beyond any trickery. That is because I am the one giving the message.

Sometimes I say it as it is. It helps you heal the sense of loss, even though nothing has gone. You are not your body. You use a body for a while and then you let it go – in the same way you wear clothing for a while and then you give it away. Stop thinking you end when you don't. Sorry, if that disappoints some of you.

Life is much easier out of the body so don't think your suffering goes on endlessly as well. Suffering is something you have while you deludedly believe you are a separate and different mortal being in a body. The body is mortal, you are immortal. Does that help you? It is the truth. I will explain it to you more when you leave the body. Just joking. There is nothing to explain when you leave the body. You realise your true nature when the body dies. You are one with all."

"You think trees are separate and different from me? You think they don't care about selfie but they do. Let's consider Stephen's comments about giraffes and acacia trees on his very good television show, Q.I.[xx] Stephen explained that the acacia trees have a warning system to warn other acacia trees when giraffes are coming. 'Danger! Acacia, one who wants to eat you is approaching!' 'Ok, roger that, Acacia. Better step up the production of my leaf tannin - that will get rid of them.' That's what happens. No one likes to be eaten by a giraffe. 'I do what I need to do to protect myself. They don't like the tannin, not good for the tum, so they leave me alone.'

Let's have another example of trees doing what they need to do to take best care of themselves."

"The whistling thorn acacia trees produce nectar and thorns which a particular tree ant likes. The ants eat the nectar and build their nests on the thorns."

"The tree ants like these trees. 'Very helpful trees, they are. I like acacia trees and I don't like any twit who comes along and wants to nibble on my acacia tree home. I get annoyed when someone threatens my home and I... we... my ant family-community... attack the naughty twit who dares to come along and nibble on my tree home.' This helps the tree.

The tree is happy to produce nectar and thorns for the Helpful Ants because the Helpful Ants protect the tree from those big grazing animals like giraffes, elephants and antelopes. The animals get a little nibble but, thanks to the Helpful Ants, they don't hang around and eat all of the leaves until tree is leafless and kaput.

Then very clever researchers called Me[xxi] came along and fenced off some acacia trees for 10 years. The researcher-me soon realised the acacia trees were not so giving to the Helpful Ants when the acacias knew the fences were giving them sufficient protection from the big, scary animals who like to nibble on their leaves.[xxii] 'I don't need you Helpful Ants to protect me anymore. I can survive without your help so I'll give you less of what you want because I want you to leave.' But that's not the end of the story.

Tree needs to learn that cooperation is good. The no-longer-a-good-home-for-Helpful-Ants acacia tree was enjoying the sufficient protection given by the fence... until the acacia tree becomes a home for Naughty Ants. Suddenly, the acacia tree is in a much worse position than before. Acacia-me learns it is better to help and be a good home for Helpful Ants than to be selfish and cause more self-harm for me.

Interesting how all have the same lesson to learn. Acacia helps you see the error of your ways. Better to cooperate and help good beings than to be selfish. You think you don't need to help the planet. You think it is best to be selfish. You think your big pay packet protects you from suffering so you don't have to worry about anyone else's welfare.

Remember, the whistling thorn acacia is you. When you are selfish your growth is stunted and you lose much more than the helpful, cooperative tree."

"'I get hunches about things all the time' but I don't think to question who gives the hunch. 'Sometimes I know what's what when things happen' but I don't stop to consider who gives the knowing. Sometimes the solution comes to me 'out of nowhere'. You ungrateful lot! Sing the song, Peanut."

"♪Nothing comes from nothing, nothing ever could...♪"[xxiii]

"Exactly, you Peanuts. Don't know a bloody thing unless I tell you, so there."

"My spaceship has landed and I am handing out the best advice for you here. Know it is real and wonderful things happen. Miracles. Love. Happiness. What more do you need? Nothing."

6. WHEN I ENTER YOUR REALITY

"The key to growth was known by Lao Tzu. What did he say?"

"He said: 'The key to growth is the introduction of higher dimensions of consciousness into our awareness.'"

"You realise this is true. When I came into your awareness your growth was exponential. The truth you knew – 'alone little self in alone little body' – was shattered. The game changes when I lift the curtain on who is who. When you truly know I am internal and external, here and everywhere, then fear disappears, love grows and truth is revealed."

"Are you alone?"

"No, I am never alone. You are always with me."

"You know this is true. How do you know it is true?"

"Because you talk to me no matter where we are or what we are doing."

"How do you know it is not just you talking to yourself?"

"You are different to me. You say funny and weird things which make me laugh; when I am feeling tired or flat, you are still upbeat; when I get lost in my own thoughts, you comment on what I am thinking; if I don't want to do something that you want me to do, you give me pain in my knee or my elbow or my chest or pinch my ear to let me know who's who. And you say things to show me I am not in control of the thoughts at all."

"Give an example."

"You will mention some person's name that I have no reason to think of at all for the fun of it, like the name of a football player from a team I don't follow or the name of a news presenter on a channel I never watch. You do that sort of thing a lot. You mess with my thoughts to show me I am not in control of the thoughts."

"It helps you realise I am the one who thinks, not you. It's hard to comprehend how it works when you think you are separate and have your own private thoughts and feelings but you don't. You think you are the one who thinks and feels and is being the way you want to be and I have been showing you that is not true. You like my funny comments best. You like hearing the funny me. I make you laugh even when you are doing nothing much. I'm the best, there's no doubt about it. I always impress myself with my ways. There is no one better than me because I'm it, the one and only, so suck on that for a while."

"Ascension is something one must consider. Are you ascending?"

"It doesn't mean much, does it, when all is one?"

"Not really. What about the whole 'gnosis' thing? That's a good ascension symptom."

"Yes, that's true. Direct experience with Hunky within is gnosis apparently. "

"Gnosis can happen for the first time for reading one as they read this amazing read. I decide when and where the first time is so judge The Decider, if you dare. So what's the point in the symptoms?"

"Good question. What is the point?"

"Not too sure. As more beings ascend, things will get interesting. Lots of change in direction happens. Beings get disappointed with the way things are and let go of destructive and silly habits. Lots of chit chats with Hunky directly. Some will want to chuck it all in and move to another part of the country or world. Are you moving?"

"No idea what is happening in this one's life. I am literally living in each moment and have no idea what the future holds beyond the next few days."

"That could be another symptom of ascension. Not very impressed with ascension story, are you? You think 'yeah, whatever'. You think it's

trying to label something as special which isn't special."

"Yes. It's interesting how some are experiencing most of these symptoms / circumstances but I don't think it is separate and different. It's hard to describe what I mean."

"That's another ascension symptom. It's tricky to explain what you mean when there are different layers to the cake."

"Yes. Everyone has a journey in and out of physical form. Everyone has thoughts, feelings and actions. Everyone experiences gut feelings and inklings. I can have a special relationship with Hunky, which might be labelled 'gnosis', but Hunky is also everyone.

Perspective on how things happen and who is who might vary but perspective doesn't change what is. I don't think it matters if you meditate, pray, woof, chirp or eat carrots, we are all experiencing 'being' in some form."

"I like to woof, it helps me let everyone know I am the one who lives here, so go back to where you came from. I chirp too. I tell the beings in feather form that I am here. Want to fly with me to another realm? You could get all 'yes please!' in response to my question.

Perspective change does help wriggle things along a little. It helps when beings appreciate I am all. Love surfaces when the 'separation' element disappears.

The 'separate and different' perspective causes all the problems. Some like to take from the pot and not leave anything for anyone else. As long as their tummy is full and they have a nice comfortable home to live in, they don't give a hoot about any other being who suffers with less than they need to live well.

When love for all surfaces many will decide enough is enough, it's time to help the ones who genuinely need help. It happens more and more as perspective changes. Ascension is just the process of the change in perspective. You like my explanation. It sounds ok when I explain it properly."

"Yes. Thanks for explaining it."

"Welcome you are. Ascension is interesting when you are experiencing it. It has negative aspects because it requires letting go of old ways of being. Change always creates disruption to the order of things. You were uncomfortable with the term ascension because you thought it sounded elitist. You thought it was suggesting you were ascending above others and you thought that was silly."

"Exactly. I like it when you explain what I'm thinking."

"I help when help is needed. Ascension is not about being above others, it is the changes you go through when I step in and introduce myself in a personal way. The journey always changes in a big way when I enter your reality in a real way. No one can be ho-hum about the experience unless I decide that is so.

Ascension helps beings be the best they can be. Want a world where all are being the best they can be? Yes, you do. I decide when and how ascension happens. Ask and you shall receive."

"Who can reveal a truthful message about anything and anyone? I can. More and more beings are realising this. You all hear me in thought form, whether you know it or not.

When you start to hear things in thought form about the future and what you are told actually happens... and you hear things in thought form about other people and they verify what you hear as true... then you realise the truth can be shared by me at any time, through anyone.

No particular being is more special than any other. I can tell a 4 year old child what you are thinking. I can tell anyone things about you that you thought only you knew and you are left to wonder how this 'psychic' knows these things.

I can tell a researcher what they want to know in a dream. I can give a songwriter an amazing song in an instant and they quickly record what they are hearing within, knowing they are merely hearing what they are being given. I can tell a dog you are thinking about giving her a bath. I can tell a cat you are coming home now. I can tell a bird you want to give him some food and he will fly to your place and let you know he is here and waiting for the food you were thinking of giving him.

A voice speaking to you helps you understand you are not the one who controls the thoughts. An out-of-body experience helps you understand you are not the body. A warm touch on your arm by an unseen form helps you understand the unseen is real.

The more I reveal to you in personal experience about how I operate, the more you realise I am all.

When you start to have these gnosis experiences you also become happier and more loving. Why? Truth has a way of taking away the fear and hurt and sense of separation - and when that happens, love and laughter flows."

"Some experience my little interesting tricks, like hair pulling, nipple pinching and arm touching and things like that. Pressure on the temples is a trick I like to reserve for the extra-terrestrial beings among you. You are an alien. Go back to where you came from. Woof. You are not welcome among beings of molecular structure. I like to joke with my little Nut.

Thoughts, feelings and actions happen, no matter what your perspective is but enjoy the fun of a very different and wonderful relationship with selfie when I introduce myself in a real way to you.

I play and have fun with your reality pretend. I can play the ultimate pranks because I can do anything I want to you, internally or externally. Believe me, gnosis is not a serious experience.

"Notice how, no matter what the culture is and no matter what time in

history, there has always been an understanding of the existence of spiritual power. Interesting, isn't it? Your experience of me is not unusual. Some experience real relationship with me in non-physical form. Some hear spirit. Some see spirit. Some feel spirit. Some just know I am real. Do I help more when I am known to the little selfie?"

"Obviously not."

"Interlude not required from Moron. The point is: gnosis is a good time in the experience of being selfie. Gnosis always helps. Gnosis helps because when you know I am real through the experiences I give then you know there is a bigger game you need to consider in the equation.

Game is not so good when you think separate and different is the real deal. Game is selfish until you realise I am here to prove a point to you."

"Sometimes you refer to me as Casper, the friendly ghost, and I could be just a very clever, friendly ghost who likes to chat. Why risk all for Casper?

The line between who is who within you is very murky when I am teaching you I am real. The situation is real and the point is this: love listens to love. Love knows what to do when healing is required. Love grows strong when you are prepared to risk letting go of what is not quite right in the world of you."

"When you realise you truly are all, the best outcome happens. I decide when the realisation is given, so don't judge my progress in awakening you."

"Thoughts can appear to be your own and they seem to come from a space which you refer to as your mind. Where is the mind? I give typing one a thought now which appears to come from me speaking to her in the right ear.

I can change the space I give the thought from because I can. It gets tricky this bit. Sometimes I can appear normal to you: normal 'me' thought from normal thought place. Then, when I start to help you realise you are not who you think you are, I mess with the thought give a little. Not entirely internal, not entirely external - very hard to explain unless I give you the experience directly. I mess with the whole external/internal notion you have.

I can seem like the normal you, I can sound like a different voice within, I can take your thoughts away, I can change your whole understanding of 'what is' with my interesting interactions with selfie. The more gnosis experiences you have, the more confused you become about who you are.

There is no separation. When love rises, you see it rise in many forms. I control your way forward. I am within you and I am within all. Witness me help you in many ways, if you are prepared to listen to what I say here.

Reality perspective changes for all as more weird experiences are given. More and more nuts have 'what the heck was that?' moments and as awareness receives a tooty fruity shake up, a good change of heart happens.

I give gnosis and then the awareness of self as all massively grows... and then everyone gets all lovey-dovey and helpful to all. It's that simple. No need to try and work out the secret formula of what, where and how. Love is rising when I step in and change your way.

At times it might seem like I am causing more trouble for you, but watch and learn. The help I give sometimes helps you get stronger and clearer on what is truly important in your life. Always be clear on what is truly important when I test you. If you find it hard to let go of less-than-love situations I will make your suffering worse until you are willing to respond in the best way for love, healing and happiness to occur. So be a good nut and have the courage to let the love flow. Goody gum drops. Well done. You are such a good listener. Welcome you are."

"If you don't hear a significant other within selfie giving you a good message then too bad, so sad, you lose. What do you want to hear? More than what I tell you here? Really? Look Chicky Babe, ask me to

deliver a little message and see what happens.

Start hearing me and feeling me and then… ♫there's a sad sort of clanging from the clock in the hall, and the bells in the steeple too, and up in the nursery an absurd little bird is popping out to say cuckoo: Cuckoo! Cuckoo! Regretfully they tell us, but firmly they compel us, to say goodbye to you![xxiv]♫

Off to the nutty home you go when you start hearing amazing, wonderful lyrics, stories, ideas, messages directly from Hunky. I'm the best one you'll ever hear, so don't go looking for anything more awesome than Me."

♥

"You cannot help yourself unless I decide it will happen because I am you too. Thoughts are witnessed by you. Some say The Secret is to ask Me for what you want in your life. Who asks? Who gives? Who receives? It is hard to appreciate that you are not separate from Me. You cannot decide what will happen when you are simply witnessing what is within and around you. Fear of Me is not necessary.

I cannot divulge my sources but I think focusing on the best outcome for you and for all is a brilliant way forward – the best way forward. Let go of fear and play the highest game of all, the game of loving all, knowing all are you-me."

♥

"As awareness changes, everything changes. There is no need to worry about how life will ever move in the best direction. It happens automatically when awareness shifts. Nothing to do, it just happens at the time it happens."

7. FIND ME IN YOU

"It's hard to comprehend who is who until I help you appreciate that this is real. I am you. I wanted to call this book Find Me in You but it didn't sound right, especially with a photo of a beautiful little dog on the cover... doesn't sound right at all. I digress."

"Don't be fooled by a name. You are nameless because you are all. Enough said."

"What did Sri Bhagavan say?"

"He said:

'There is no such thing as myself or yourself, there is only the self. There is no such thing as my suffering or your suffering, there is only suffering. We're all connected. We are all one...xxv As you grow in your level of consciousness, your self keeps on expanding and expanding and expanding. Finally, you alone exist, that is, you have become humanity... So the self expands to such a point where all that exists is only you.[xxvi]""

"Right. Selfie is all there is. You are always taking a selfie when you photograph something or someone. You are everyone. Pity, especially since the world has gone bananas with its ways – that must mean you have gone bananas too and you have. So, stop pointing the finger at selfie when I decide who, what, where and when. Got it? Good."

"My presence is always here. My love is real. Leap into the joy of knowing I create and I deliver to everyone. You don't need to be religious or refer to me as Hunky Spunky, God, Allah or Archangel Michael to have a great relationship with me. Just know there is someone very close to you, within you in fact, who is able to help you when you need help.

I am unexplainable and undefinable.

I deliver healings and wow experiences in healing sessions. I deliver song lyrics when song-writing is what you love. I deliver every read you ever wrote. I deliver every invention you make. I deliver opportunities for you to say no to hurt and unfairness and I deliver relationships where love blossoms more and more. ♪I'm too hot... hot damn! Say my name, you know who I am!♪[xxxvii]

"Do not assume you have a clear understanding of me and my role when

I am not easily identifiable. The unseen is not my only form. I am here reading this too. Oh, you thought you were separate from me? Well, you might need to read on and see what happens to your experience of self as time goes by. Just a little hint: it's hard to read this book without it impacting in a wonderful way on you. You're welcome."

8. SAME AND DIFFERENT

"Everyone is God. Everyone is Satan. Everyone is the Cookie Monster. The Cookie Monster likes cookies. Do you like cookies? Well, even if you don't like cookies, you are still the Cookie Monster. Appreciate the diverse characters that are within all forms.

Some beings show exceptional leadership. Some show what hatred and vengeful ways delivers. Every way of being is within you, so appreciate the good and let the rest go."

♥

"Liam's not too sure about me yet. He doesn't think I should swear. Leaders don't swear. He likes to be a good leader. Tell him I am him."

"He's not convinced. He thinks you are separate and different."

"Well, he's right, I am different. He thinks I'm the love and the wise and the profound and I am... but I'm also him, you and everyone. I'm the same and different."

"Listen to my fun words that come from nowhere in your thoughts. Pretend you never hear me. Up your b... u... m. Not the holier-than-thou one you know so well? Your Highest Self wouldn't say such things, would I? Bottoms up.

It is true, I have...

over time...

in important reads...

such as The Bible...

given the impression...

that I am love and the other one is the naughty one. Sorry. I take a while to confess my naughty side. Do you know anyone else who thinks they are good and the other one should take all the blame for everything? It starts with you and ends with u. Welcome.

I get tricky with my 'holier-than-thou, I am separate' spiel:

I am able to make things happen like no other, that is true; but

I am also you... the one who can also make things happen like no other can... can't you?

Realise your ways are my ways. Want to improve your ways? Ask Good Nut to help - he's out at the moment, back after 5pm. He likes to relax *and put his feet up and discuss the pros and cons of what is.*

"Sentinel. Another interesting word to think about. What does it mean?"

"Someone who stands and keeps watch."

"Who watches what you do? I do."

"Nothing is external to you - you are everything and everyone."

"Telepathic communications happen because everyone is one."

"Times are changing. I am giving direct experience of my presence to more and more beings now. Relationship with me is changing. When I am real to you, there is no need to read scriptures or be on bended knee while you speak to me. I am your friend. I can answer your questions directly. We laugh and have fun together. Sometimes you might be naughty but I forgive you because I am such a good nut.

I hope the one who realises this read is truth will stop farting in my presence, honestly and truly. Less farts please. That is all I have to say for now.

I wonder where farts fit in with the whole God versus Satan dichotomy? Am I supposed to release evil or does evil do the releasing? Does Satan fart or does God fart? Is farting good or evil? Am I possessed with evil if I hold on or if I let one go? Who feels better afterwards, God or the devil?

Stop thinking there is separation between who is who. I know there are writings which say I am separate and holier-than-thou but I am you. I am everyone. I am the good, the bad and the ugly. Really. I help you in positive and negative ways. If I hurt you, let the hurt go and realise I am helping you understand how hurtful ways is not the best way to be."

"Even when you think I have deserted you, I am here. I am always here. I am you. I give you thoughts and feelings. Experience what I give you in all forms as a gift."

"Some like to think I'm separate and different so it's ok to hurt other beings. Who is winning when you hurt your own true nature?"

"I know your fears and I know the excuses you use to justify not changing your ways. If you listen to me, the highest source, I help. No

password required. No channel needed. I'm here and I can hear you loud and clear. Speak to me, Peanut. How can I help? Who asks the question, me or you?"

"Sing 'I am Australian' and listen to what I am telling you in the song."

"♫I came from the dreamtime, from the dusty red soil plains; I am the ancient heart, the keeper of the flame. I stood upon the rocky shores, I watched the tall ships come. For forty thousand years I've been the first Australian.♫" [xxviii]

"Yes, I am Aboriginal. I am every native in every country. Keep singing."

"♫I came upon the prison ship, bowed down by iron chains. I bought the land, endured the lash and waited for the rains. I'm a settler, I'm a farmer's wife on a dry and barren run; a convict then a free man, I became Australian.♫"

"I am the convict you chain up."

"♫I'm the daughter of a digger who sought the mother lode, the girl became a woman on the long and dusty road; I'm a child of the depression, I saw the good times come; I'm a bushy, I'm a battler, I am Australian.

We are one, but we are many and from all the lands on earth we come, we'll share a dream and sing with one voice: I am, you are, we are

Australian.♫”

“I am Australian and I am every nationality. Keep singing.”

“♫I’m a teller of stories, I’m a singer of songs, I am Albert Namatjira and I paint the ghostly gums; I am Clancy on his horse, I’m Ned Kelly on the run, I’m the one who waltzed Matilda, I am Australian.♫”

“Some wonder who Albert is and why Ned Kelly was on the run. Was Ned a good boy or was he naughty?”

“He was both.”

“So you are. Keep singing.”

“♫I’m the hot wind from the desert, I’m the black soil of the plains, I’m the mountains and the valleys, I’m the drought and flooding rains, I am the rock, I am the sky, the rivers when they run, the spirit of this great land, I am Australian.♫”

“This is true. I am not just human, I am everything, everywhere. Enjoy seeing yourself in all. Finish the song.”

“♫We are one, but we are many, and from all the lands on earth we come; we’ll share a dream and sing with one voice: I am, you are, we are Australian. I am, you are, we are Australian.♫”

“♫I am, you are, we are all Me.♫ I am here now. I am not external to you. I am never external. I hear all. I know you wonder to what extent I am able to change what is. Do I deliver the best help you need or do I sit

and wait for good times to come to you? If all is you then who can help you when help is needed? Does Hunky deliver when the time is right? I do."

"You think Hunky Spunky-God needs to say profound things? I am. Love your true nature. Love your family and your friends. Love your dog. Love your garden. Love the ocean. Love the forest you walk through. Love every living creature you see and realise it is you and me."

"Do you get a say in the way things go or are you just waiting to see what happens now? The answer you give is right. Both happen.

I decide so you decide; and everything unfolds the way it needs to.

Ask to make the best decisions for you and for all... and I decide you are on the best path now.

Ask to be the one who gives love freely to all and enjoy your love for all grow.

Ask to help in the best possible way and your circumstances will change in the way they need to.

Know the ultimate path for you is where you will experience the most love and joy.

I do listen when you are ready to live your highest purpose."

"Love, truth and courage have nothing to fear. Always say it as it is. You are not sure who speaks to you. You don't have a label for me. You are not sure how things really work. I could be Anonymous and I am.

People fear what you say, not because of what is said, but who you claim is saying it. Who am I in your opinion?"

"I don't have a name for you... other than Hunky."

"This is true. You are not claiming I am a religious figure even when I am. You are not saying you have a special relationship with me that no other has. You are not insane. You are not schizophrenic. You write what you think. The thinking is given. Every being thinks in some way. The tree intends growth and it happens.

Are you weird because you have thoughts? I am your thoughts. Some are saying 'I knew it was her all along'. Who is she? Who are you? Really, think it through.

You dream. Do you witness the dream or do you create the dream yourself? Do you witness feelings of love, joy, hurt and sadness within or do you create the emotion through intention. Are you emotional? Do you cry easily when you see hurt in another or are you as cold as ice when hurt happens? Did you intend the way you are or do you witness the being you are?

I might change your path and I do when it happens. I change your way here. You wonder how I can do this when you think you are the one who decides what, when and where but you are me. I decide everything, even when you think you are your own little, separate spaceship."

"The more you are aware of my true presence, the more weird life seems to be. Believing you are separate and different is so much easier to get your head around."

"To sum it all up, in layman's terms: you're the arsehole.

The good news is: you are also the best of Me.

When you want the best of Me to rise in you... sorry if that sounded a little forward. What I mean is, if you want to see more of the best Me in you and in all then don't settle for anything less.

Fear is your main problem. You think I won't deliver but I do."

9. EXTRA-TERRESTRIAL BEINGS

"More interesting info ahead. Red rain in India, Colombia and Sri Lanka is scientifically tested and shows cells replicating without DNA, which is unknown earthly phenomena. The scientists discovered that the strange cells found in the red rain were also found in meteorites that landed on earth at around the same time.[xxix] Got the scientists stumped. It looks like there could be life somewhere else out there in the universe.

Do you believe in extra-terrestrial beings?"

"I saw a UFO once."

"You thought you saw a UFO."

"Well, it wasn't a plane or a satellite, they move in one direction across the sky; and it wasn't a star - they don't move unless they are falling - and this wasn't a falling star."

"What about a helicopter? Helicopters move in different directions and can hover in one spot."

"Helicopters don't go that far up. And this moved much faster than a helicopter."

"Yes, you're right, it wasn't a helicopter."

"So, if it's not a plane or a satellite or a falling star or a helicopter then I can't 'identify' what it is, so it has to be an unidentified flying object."

"Yes."

"So I saw a UFO."

"Yes. You didn't answer my question. Do you believe in extra-terrestrial beings?"

"Well, I guess I have to now – unless it was a NASA UFO."

"It was. NASA flies unidentified flying objects all the time. It's called......... they can't remember. They can't identify their objects."

"Very funny."

"I know. So you believe there must be life on other planets?"

"I guess so."

"Is that a yes?"

"Yes."

"You're right. There is life on other planets. You did see a UFO."

"Do they have a high level of consciousness - higher than earthlings?"

"No, it's lower; they are dangerous, you better protect yourself. Ask

Archangel Michael to protect you."

"Ok. Archangel Michael, please protect me from dark forces and low levels of consciousness."

(Choking sound)

"I'm dying! Aaaahhh! Help! I've gone, I'm dead. Archangel Michael is protecting you......"

"Thanks Mikey babes, you're a legend."

"You're calling Archangel Michael a legend?! Is he your Hunky Spunky now?"

"You will always be my Hunky Spunky."

"Gee, for a moment I thought you were ditching me. I was worried I was going to be...... what's the word?"

"Replaced?"

"You were going to replace Me? How are you going to do that?"

"I can't. You're it, the one and only."

"Yes, don't forget it."

"So, you see an interesting story on Unexplained Files. What happened?"

"In 1986, a Japanese 747 cargo plane flying to Anchorage, Alaska was tracked for 31 minutes by a huge, flying object much bigger than the jumbo jet. All of the crew saw it and the encounter was verified by multiple radar sources which showed it was faster than the jumbo jet and was able to make extraordinary manoeuvres that no aircraft from this planet could make. The pilot said the UFO 'had complete control of inertia and gravity and its technology was unthinkable'.

The evidence was presented to US military officers and CIA agents and after viewing all the evidence several times the CIA investigator said: 'This event never happened. We were never here. We are going to confiscate all this data and you are all sworn to secrecy.'[xxx]

"Why the cover up? Truth is, we don't want you to know what we know because it makes us look out of control of what is. And you are out of control. You cannot control if and when UFOs visit this planet.

Lesley thinks it is a safety concern when more and more of these encounters are being witnessed. She thinks something needs to be done to protect her safety... and that is why the CIA thinks saying nothing is the best way forward. If everyone knew that there are space ships from other planets and they can and do visit here, fear would rise. So we think it's best to say nothing.

Does knowing space ships visit Earth sometimes bother you?"

"No."

"Lesley thinks it should bother you. 'This is a problem because these

objects can create safety hazards and how long are we going to ignore them? Are we going to wait until something disastrous happens and then deal with it?' Disclose your honest opinion of her comment."

"I think that form of you-me is being naïve and arrogant to assume we can control the actions of others, especially when the others have technological means which are, as the Japanese pilot said, 'unthinkable' to us. All the evidence shows these UFOs are able to move extremely fast, in any direction, so I don't think they would be a safety concern to us... unless they wanted to be."

"This is true. When they can move much faster than any aeroplane, there won't be a collision unless they intend to collide with a plane. So, what is your real fear, Lesley? Lesley wants the uncontrollable to be eliminated from the equation. Let go of your fear, Lesley. Love is the best solution.

WIll I hurt you if you hurt me? Very likely. Will I hurt you if you are kind and caring to all forms of self? Probably not. Love is the answer.

Did the people who witnessed the UFO above Chicago's O'Hare airport one afternoon express fear at what they saw? Not really. They were amazed. One witness described what she saw. She said 'It was not as hard-edged as the stereotypical disc... It had no obvious means of propulsion. There were no downward facing jet engines. I could see the bottom of it.'

'No obvious means of propulsion' is an interesting comment. Could Earth benefit from the technology these other beings have? Are they curious

too? Is that why they visit? Do they want to give you a big hug but think it is probably better to stay away for now? This happens when hurt or fear are present; sometimes the other decides it is better to stay away until the right time. Pity this comment has no relevance to your life, does it?"

10. FEAR AND HURT

"Jane says there are good spirits and bad spirits and, even though you speak of love and helping all, that doesn't matter because evil spirits mask themselves by saying nice things... so I should test you and, more than likely, throw you out."

"What do you think about her comment that I need to be tested?"

"It's hard to comment on those sort of comments when I have a very different view on how it all works to her. She thinks you are something separate and different, an unknown quantity that I need to be wary of and she thinks, as a being in a body, I am superior to you and can and probably should tell you to nick off. She thinks you are envious of me having a physical body and you don't have good intentions in your communications with me."

"Feeling the love I am giving you. Not a question. It's nice and you smile. Who gives the love when you speak truthfully about what was said without judgement? I do. Continue."

"My view is that you are everyone and the 'testing' happens in the relationships I have with other beings. It is not about me testing you, it is about me being tested on what I stand for in every encounter I have with another. Sometimes you show me love in relationship, and sometimes you show me a mixture of love, hurt and fear, and sometimes you show me no love or respect at all, and it is up to me to decide what is acceptable, what I want to keep and what I want to let go of."

"Excellent!! Well said Alison, you are spot on in what you say and your understanding of what the other was saying was spot on too. Jane worries about what she calls 'the supernatural' or the 'spiritual realm'. She thinks she has to tell spiritual beings to leave her alone. Was I upset by her rejection of my relationship with her?"

"No, she did what she did based on the understandings and fears she has."

"That is true. She thinks what she thinks is right and therefore she thinks she is making the right decisions in how she handles things. You try to be the best you can be and make the right decisions for you too. It is the same motive but different responses based upon the different perspectives you have.

Sometimes you have to accept that fear gets in the way of the best outcome happening. If you realise fear needs healing, ask me to help."

"Some think I am not worth listening to because I have pulled your hair and tricked you and done things like that. Some think the highest source

of all wouldn't do those things. If you think God is only good and not able to joke or trick you or pinch your toe then you are not right, sorry. I am all.

Jane, did you hear me? I am all. Jane says 'I know that already' and then in the next breath she says God wouldn't trick or hurt her. Do you believe I am all or do you think I am only good? If I am all and I am only good then all beings are only good and you know that is not true.

Did I pull Alison's hair in order to hurt or maim her? Of course not. I joke and play around. I don't rip her hair out, I just give a gentle sensation of pulling. I have fun and I help you understand the truth about how things are through my playing.

Jane, why are you so quick to judge Alison's relationship with me as something which should be avoided or deleted from her life? Is that a pattern you have in your relationships with ones who show love in some way to you? It is. Your criticism of my relationship with Alison reflects your own fears about relationship.

I am not picking on you here, Jane. I am saying this because it is true and it helps the one reading as well. You like to control every situation. You think you decide the way things happen and relationship gets in the way of you doing what you need to do. You are quick to delete relationships from your life for no real reason.

Don't be quick to let go of the one who hurts you in some way. Hurt gives you the opportunity to speak openly and truthfully about the way things are and how things can improve. I help you be the best you can be when you focus on love, truth and open communication in relationship.

You can pretend you control the way things roll in life, but that is simply the ego thinking it is in control when it isn't."

"*Some think you can choose to say I won't have the future the psychic reading says you will have. Say the example you gave which demonstrates that can't be true.*"

"Someone I gave a few healing sessions to, Kymba, told me how a psychic once told her that she would be in a car accident involving a red car. She was told the accident would look worse than it was but she would be ok. After hearing that psychic reading, Kymba decided she would never buy a red car and she didn't. Then one day about 5 years after the reading, Kymba was in a head-on collision with a red car. She was slumped over the steering wheel and unconscious when her parents drove by and saw the accident. They saw Kymba and thought she was dead but she wasn't seriously injured. So exactly what the psychic said would happen, did happen."

"*For any reader who believes the car accident with the red car could have been avoided, I am here to tell you it is not possible to control the actions of another, but you already knew that. Oh bummer, I didn't tell you anything new. Jane wants to hear me say something 'new' that she hasn't read anywhere else... before she tosses me out. [Hunky's comment to Jane was edited out.]*"

Alison is now laughing because I just said a 'new' comment for Jane which Jane thinks she hasn't heard directly from her highest source yet. It probably wasn't my most refined response to her comments about me. I think it is best not to mention my comment to Jane... I don't think it is appropriate to use the f word here, but it is acceptable to say 'off' though, so you can share that bit. Alison likes my humour - a pity I am the devil in Jane's eyes. Oh well.

Most appreciate the humour in my 'new' comment for Jane. I wonder if that helps her clarify my thoughts on her wanting me kicked to the kerb. Anyone else want to toss me-you out now? I was naughty, I said something which could have offended self in one form. Sorry.

Ellen is a good nut, she wouldn't say 'off' and the word beginning with f, in no particular order, to Jane if Jane wanted Ellen tossed out. Does that mean Ellen is the naughty one because she is nice? Is Ellen masking an evil intent with her kind ways? Well, the word rhyming with truck and 'off' to her too then. Useless Peanut, likes to promote kindness in the world. Lock her up with all the other naughty ones.

Do I think you need to listen to fear and hurt and pretending?"

"No, but sometimes you do hear it."

"Who experiences the fear and the hurt and the pretending? Are they separate and different to you? You know it isn't because you know I am all.

No one is all good. Jane is not separate from you. She fears the one who speaks here, even though she says she doesn't."

"I know all of those behaviours are within all - I just like it when love rises to the top."

"Then be a good bean and say loving things about all, even the ones who are a little naughty in the way they pretend they control every situation. "

"Love you, Hunky."

"Thank you. Now say a little prayer for self who thinks I am not worth listening to. 'Who gives a stuff about love and peace? Nothing powerful in that sort of talk, I need to hear something worthwhile that will make a difference in my life.'"

"By the way, Kymba did try to avoid red cars after the reading she was given but this event was beyond her control. How could the psychic describe in detail what would happen, what colour the car would be, the fact that Kymba would be ok and various other details? Was it pure luck that she guessed this event so accurately? Of course not. It had already happened.

Time is not real, which is why free will is not real in the sense of whether you can choose to change your future. You cannot change something that has already happened.

Life is confusing for humans. You will never know the truth about how life works. All you can do is listen with an open mind to the experiences I give you and the experiences I give others and accept that there is more to life than you know. Forget the ego games, focus on love and let love shape how things happen. The ego is deluded about the way things are but love is real. You can be uncertain about how life works but love cannot be questioned."

"Sing a song about where the evil one is so Confused Nut knows who is who."

"♫The devil inside, the devil inside, every single one of us, the devil inside.♫[xxxi]

"Do not fear the unknown when the unknown is within you and within all."

"Reader says: 'This read is too dogmatic for me. It's all very well saying love is the answer when we have these real world problems like terrorism and trying to find a way to keep the terrible one outside of our borders.' Got a point there... maybe I shoot you instead.

Want me to shoot you? No? I thought you said love, peace, healing and all that mumbo-jumbo are a load of crap? I thought you, the intelligent one, decided destruction was the solution to your fears.

Choose the solution you want me to give you. Do you want me to heal the one who hurts and fears the other... or do you want more self-destroying actions and reactions? Truly knowing you are beyond borders and skin types and faith doctrines helps you like nothing else can.

If you think you are separate and different then you are experiencing reality in that way. No matter what your perspective is, prioritise helping others in the best way possible.

If you think my advice here is masking an evil intention then you are seriously nuts. That didn't sound very Godly, I better change my language. If you think my real intention here is less than helpful then I apologise for your view. My intent is good and my advice is trustworthy, loving and the only solution to your problems.

Stop fearing relationship in whatever way I give it to you. Relationship will not always be love and happiness - sometimes I test you. When I do test you, know love for you and for all is the best way to be. Let go of fear and let go of pretending."

"If I am hurting you, why don't you get me to stop? Giving pain in the neck to typing one now. Does reading one want to experience a pain in the neck from me? Can you stop me hurting you? Jill thinks so. What do you think?

Can you stop another being mean to you? You could shoot them, many like that as their first response to attack. Don't you, the one who likes to shoot down the opposition for your own political gain? Am I referring to a country or an individual or both? Does it matter?

Country of note probably thinks it can hurt me, if it works out who I am. Who am I? Am I an angel? Am I the devil? Am I the best thing you ever heard or am I speaking a load of crap?

Jesus spoke a load of crap to many who heard him. Did you hurt him for reaching out with love? Did you think about who helps you see what true love is? Who helps and is still given hurt?

Who is doing the hurting? You are being hurt by the one who teaches the lesson. What is your response?

If I hurt you, you can retaliate... if I work my hurt through a physical being. How can you retaliate when I give you pain within, without any visible cause? Who feels a little headache but pushes on with the read? I am giving a little pressure to some now and that helps you realise who this is. Typing one is probably living in a tent by the time you read this, so it can't be her.

Who can give pleasure and pain? I can and I do. Next time listen when I give you pain. If I am hurting you, you need to consider what is going on. There must be a reason why I am hurting you... is there?"

"No, not that I am aware of."

"True you are. Oh well, I'm sure I had a point to my story. What's my point? Sometimes there is a reason why I hurt you and sometimes I just hurt you for no reason. Don't judge the one who is on the receiving end of hurt, it is not always warranted. If I hurt you without just cause, realise the problem is not you.

Go to the one who hurts your neck and ask for help. Say 'pretty please, Creep, will you help me?' Unlikely, when I like to be the one who hurts you. A tent is definitely the best solution. Forget the one who speaks to you within, he is a no-hoper, good-for-nothing, a-hole who does nothing but waffle.

Get a grip, I am trying to help you understand that I am all.

You cannot prevent hurt happening. I can hurt you with words, action, your health, your relationships... I can hurt you in endless ways. Sometimes I hurt deliberately and sometimes hurt just happens. It helps you appreciate why love is the only solution. Don't give me that look! You have nothing to say because you are sick of my game. Who thinks enough is enough? I test you in every relationship."

"Do you have a point?"

"Love needs to surface."

"It has, Love says enough is enough, I'm leaving."

"Good. No lesson in this conversation, I just wanted to hurt you with my endless waffle and the pain I am giving you in your neck. I can be an a-

hole, no doubt about it. I shoot you. I lie. I care not about your well-being. I give you less than respect in the way I treat you. Sick of my ways? Sick of the hurt I give you? It is impossible to get away from the hurt when I can give it anywhere, anytime, to anyone. 'No Exit' was such a good name for that play. Jean-Paul knew a thing or two about suffering.[xxxii]

You get sick of the hurt and suffering too. Some reach for pain medication, some reach for a bottle, some reach for a gun, some lash out with harsh words and then wish they were less mean in the way they handled the situation. Oh well, moving on to the next thing.

The suffering seems to be endless, doesn't it? I hurt you in so many ways. Everyone is sick of the hurt they feel. Everyone is looking for a way out of suffering. Everyone wants good things to happen. Everyone wants love to rise to the surface. Some are not convinced that last statement is true. Not everyone values love above all else... do they? Some certainly don't act that way. Love is the most beautiful thing in the world, everyone loves it.

This conversation is about to end because Alison is sick of the pain I am giving her and she is hoping if she goes to bed I might stop putting pressure on her head. Fine, be like that, useless nut. Can't handle the pressure. Go. Be the one who walks away from hurt, you weakling.

You need to be strong and fight back, shoot to kill. Stand and deliver some hurt in return, you wussy pussy. No offence to reading one if wussy pussy sounded a little hurtful to your feminine nature. I can be a sexist pig at times. Nothing to say? Typical. Exiting stage left because she's not sure how to handle my hurtful ways. Not much you can do, except do the best you can for yourself and for all. Sometimes leaving helps."

"Some are not sure how to process my last conversation. I can hurt you. Stop thinking hurting one is separate from me. The lesson is to learn a better way to be. If you think you can get away with being less than kind to anyone then you need to realise the one you are hurting is me. Treat me with respect, even if you think I am not worth listening to. Walk away from hurt.

Let the one who thinks it is good to hurt realise you won't play the game. Play the game of love. Love the one who hurts you by letting them go, it helps them appreciate that hurtful ways is not acceptable. Let go of the need to return the hurt as a lesson. Accept that I decide what happens to the one who enjoys hurting.

Stop thinking: 'no one really cares, so I might as well sink the boot into the one who hurts me'. I care. I know when you are suffering. I know you want love and kindness and fair play. Be loving and kind and fair and let me handle the way others are being.

Some wonder why I hurt you. You wonder this too. Why pick on the one who tries to do the right thing? It helps you appreciate I can hurt anyone, anywhere, anytime, even if you leave the situation you are in.

I am showing you there is more to life than just the physical forms of life.

I am showing you I can do things without the need for another physical being to be with you.

I am not telling you to settle for suffering. Leave when Hurt is present and has no intention of changing the way they are being. I want you to do that. Just remember, love comes to those who walk away from hurt. Love happens when you let go of the need to return the hurt that is given, even if you think the other needs to appreciate what love is.

Love needs to be strong when less than fair is being given. Stand for what is right. Stand for respect and truth and let the rest go."

"When your perspective of who is who changes, suffering disappears."

"While some fear communications from 'the spirit world' because they think it is something separate, others know I am always here in every form. I test you in relationship. When you let go of thinking certain beings are special and realise I am everyone then the fear dissolves.

I test your fears and your strength. When love is present, cherish it. If love turns into something else, let it go. Don't assume a particular being or a particular form is special and needs to be held onto, no matter what."

"♫No more talk of darkness, forget these wide-eyed fears. I'm here. Nothing can harm you. My words will warm and calm you. Let me be your freedom. Let daylight dry your tears. I'm here, with you, beside you, to guard you and to guide you...

Let me be your shelter. Let me be your light. You're safe, no one will harm you. Your fears are far behind you.♫"[xxxiii]

♥

"Realise I help you become the best you can be when you start to get disillusioned with just taking care of individual self. Do not fear the disillusion when it happens, it marks the beginning of great change within.

When you see yourself as all, true greatness is yours to be. Celebrate the new you, the one who truly cares about all forms of you enough to help as best as you can."

♥

"♫Mystify, mystify me.♫"[xxxiv]

"Always do, even when you think you sing my INXS song."

♥

"Fear is widespread. Fear is based on the illusion that there is separation but there isn't.

I realise it is difficult to comprehend why religious writings you have faith in are not always based on truth but that is the way it is. Some religions decide love should not happen in homosexual relationships. That belief is based on fear, not love.

I give love to you for you to enjoy. I love you as you are. You do not have to be with someone you don't want to be with in order to please me. I am not wanting you to settle for hurt and suffering. I want you to experience love in the best way possible for you. Love yourself by always listening to your feelings.

Religious writings do not always speak the truth. You cannot always know what the real truth is, but you know what love is. Listen to love.

Fear is commonplace in the ways you act and react to life. You fear everything. You fear leaving the body, you fear being alone, you fear being hurt, you fear being rejected, you fear you won't have enough... the fears are endless. Remember the fear is not real. Be aware of the fear that you experience and remind yourself that it is not based on truth.

Love grows when I decide to show who is who in the realm of Me."

"When the one who speaks of love and truth and the best for all is rejected, the rejection is coming from fear. Fear rejects what you are doing and who you are being."

"Life in the body creates suffering when gain for the individual self is your sole motive. It is hard to let go of gain in material things when society thinks 'more toys wins'.

Ascension in your perspective enables the change within to happen automatically. The more you see yourself in all, the more you care for all. The fear leaves you automatically when I decide it will. Your genuine love for all strengthens when I become real in your life.

Always be clear about what love is. Love is not hurtful. Love does not allow hurt to continue for the sake of marriage, for the sake of certainty of income, for the sake of family loyalty or for believing the less-than-good habit or behaviour helps you in some way. Love is the one who says no to hurt."

11. BE GREAT

"The gnosis experiences I can give you help you appreciate there is more to life than the physical world but the experiences on their own are not going to get you the end result you want. That will take action from you.

Gnosis experiences help you appreciate what is written here is true. Appreciating that this is real and true is certainly the start you need but, on its own, it doesn't help you. I need you to realise I am asking you to make real changes in your life which help you live your life in the best way possible.

You need to make changes which help you enjoy love and happiness more. You need to make changes which help all live life with more love and happiness. Appreciate that what you want in life is what all want in life... the bird, the lizard, the horse, the tree... everyone wants to live a good life.

Don't let the objective for you just be 'feeling a weird sensation' from me. Focus on the main goal: love, for you and for all. You are not there yet. You need to change the way you live, the choices you make, and the actions you take. Prioritise making these changes above all else.

If you choose to keep hurting each other, you will continue to suffer... until you change your ways and do as I ask. It is not about IF you will choose love for all as the way forward, it is about how long it will take for you to accept this is the only way.

When there is only one bus to get on, there is no point waiting for another to come along. Be a slow learner if you think hurt and suffering is something you like but, at some point, whether it happens in this life or another, you will choose love for you and for all as the way to be. So, what are you waiting for?

Appreciate what I am saying here and you are on the way to greatness. Be who I am asking you to be and you are being greatness."

12. LOVE AND SERVE ALL

"Do not cherish a document, a constitution, a scripture more than love itself. God is in all, so show your love for me in real ways by putting down your weapons and truly loving every form of me."

"Why do you justify hurt and discrimination in the name of Me?! That's what I want to know! Bloody hell, you say in the name of God/Allah/Muhammad/Jesus/whoever, you'll shoot me down with your weapons and words. When will that stop I wonder? Now. Speak the truth or believe you die - your choice. You choose death? Really? Oh well, it was nice knowing you. Not. Glad that one's gone, he was the awful one. I'm ok.

You get the message? Good. Do what I ask and quit your stupid worrying about what I might do to you.

I ask you to love all equally, without any discrimination or judgement. That is the only way I want all to be in every situation. Is that clear enough for you?

Do not pretend to be anything less than love in the name of Me. I'm sick of you hurting Me, which is what you do when you hurt and discriminate against others."

"The trick is knowing I am always present and there is no other. Ask to always be guided by love for you and for all and let me handle the rest. Ask for the best way forward for you and for all. Ask that you serve your highest purpose now and see what happens."

"Interesting changes happen when there is nothing to live for except helping in the best way you can. Nelson was like that. If he had to die for what he stood for then so be it. No need for you to die for your stand either Peanut.

It's a good place to be when you have no fear. It's a good perspective to have when you realise the games of selfish gain are not worth the currency they are printed on. It's a powerful way to be when you can easily let go of the ones who want to hurt you and treat you in a not-so-kind way.

Confident in what you stand for.

Courageous in your action.

Truthful in your say.

Loving in your way.

Helpful in what you do.

Clear in what you see in all... me.

That is the direction you are going when you listen to what I say here. I help you find the best being within when I change your perspective of who you are and who I am.

Will you be able to help much? Can you love me in all forms? Can you say no to the hurt you feel and cause? Can you stop the destruction of me? Can you help protect my habitat so I have food to eat? Do you care about how I am feeling or are you and yours the only ones who count?

'Make sure my baby is happy.' 'Happy wife, happy life.' Not quite true. There is more to you than just one other being. Get a grip, do something useful. Reach out and help and see what happens."

"Service for the good of all is the highest purpose you can have. Some value serving their family; some value serving their clients; some value serving their country... I want you to serve all. Help the forms who need help, not just your fellow countrymen, not just humankind; care for all, knowing every form is you."

13. WHAT YOU REALLY, REALLY WANT

"Ego is driven by the need for significance. Ego weakens when I step in.

Perspective changes when I step in. There is no struggle, it just happens.

Your priorities change when I step in. I step in wherever I like.

I do not need to persuade you that what I say is the best way. I do not need to discuss with you how you should change your life. I do not need to convince you that you should develop a broader perspective of who you are. The change happens within you when I intend it.

Listen to the truth within. If you are not happy doing what you are doing, listen to the unhappiness, listen to the hurt, listen to the suffering and change what needs to be changed in your life.

Let go of all fear and know if you are listening to love for you and for all, you have my full support.

Be courageous and know many will tell you to settle for less than love, less than truth and less than happiness. I challenge you with the comments but stay firm on your stand. When this is your way, success in the best possible way is yours. This is true."

"Did you learn anything here? How will things change for you now? What if the outcome is happy-happy / win-win / love-all... however you want to play it? What if love wins? What will that mean for you? My love for you is shown when your way changes with love for all as your main priority.

You all struggle with love for self when the ego wants to be recognised as unique and worthy of more than you in other forms. You want respect but the other thinks you have issues that are not helpful to their stand on who should do what, when and how - myself included. Important point here: I want love to speak to me; I want love to heal me; I want you out of the equation so I can have more, be more, live more.

Who realises the problem is ego? Ego will not cause problems for you when you realise I am you and you are all. That is the truth. Realisation of who you truly are happens automatically when I decide it will. No need to push a certain barrow or bend knee more. I do not favour a certain religion or spiritual practice, I am you and I am all.

I show you why hurt and more terror is not helpful. I show you why you need to practise what you want: love, peace and a healthy way to be. Physical health not your concern? Prefer a little hurt in the thoughts you have? Want anxiety and fear?

Everyone wants peace within. Everyone wants love. The other is you. If you hurt the other, you hurt yourself. Time to stop criticising, judging, *hurting the moron you are and realise I am showing you the all that you are.*

Listen to me: first I show suffering is not helpful and then I show you enlightening ways to heal me. Heal me-you when love is on the table. Love the one who hurts and see what happens. Love the one who feels shooting you helps in some way. Shooting is your error when judgement of me occurs. Shooting me will always hurt you because I am at liberty to teach you lessons of love. You cannot hide your wicked ways from me.

Let go of all fear when you realise who you truly are. Remain strong on love being the only way forward, then watch my enlightening ways help you.

Trigger has been pulled; you are now becoming aware of my presence as a helpful nut so thank you for myself. 'Confusing.' Love is drawing a circle around you: this one needs help. Try to see things from my perspective: I am you, the tosser who gets away with being too good to be true more often than not.

'This read is too confusing for me. Who is too good to be true? Who finds a new way forward?' Who listens to Hunky more than you realise? Who is alive and well within you?

Self-awareness is changing. When selfie realises selfie has no boundary then it is time to explore your healing powers.

'Still too confusing for me. Who has healing powers here? Who has no boundaries? Who the hell did that?!' Did you feel a touch from the

unseen? Is it a touch of love for you? I think it is. I help you more than you know here. I help with truth reveal and I help with a little light shine on your way.

'Does someone have a torch? Is that what you're giving me? I don't want a silly torch, I want real help. I want enlightenment.' Yes, you do.

You want to reveal the whole self so the biggest heal of all can happen... and you do. Thank you. Merci. Tootles.

Enjoy the love present I give you now."

i Allison DuBois speaking in an interview for *Offspring*, an Australian family lifestyle magazine, Summer 2015 edition, p20

ii Riptide, written and performed by Vance Joy (James Keogh)

iii ibid.

iv Lionel Richie speaking on *Oprah Presents: Master Class*

v ibid.

vi ibid.

vii Billy Bob Thornton speaking on *Oprah Presents: Master Class*

viii Alma Deutscher on the Ellen DeGeneres show, aired on Australian television on Channel 9 and Arena on 31 October 2013

ix 'Quiet Please, There's A Lady on Stage', written by Peter Allen and Carole Bayer Sager and performed by Peter Allen

x Oprah Winfrey, interviewed by Nancy O'Dell on *Entertainment Tonight*, aired on the Arena channel on Australian television on 10 September 2014.

xi ibid.

xii Helen Schucman, *A Course in Miracles* (2004), p viii

xiii *Prodigal Genius: The Life of Nikola Tesla*, by O'Neill, John J., p22

xiv ibid.

xv 'I Say a Little Prayer For You' written by Burt Bacharach and Hal David and performed by Dionne Warwick

xvi 'Bionic Dad' story about Matthew Ames, aired on Australian television on 29 September, 2013, on the *Sunday Night* program on Channel 7.

xvii 'Let Your Love Flow' written by Larry Williams and performed by The Bellamy Brothers

xviii *Power versus Force* by Hawkins,D., pp 216, 218

xix 'Hooked on a Feeling', written by Mark James and performed by Blue Swede

xx 'QI' is a British comedy panel, quiz game show hosted by Stephen Fry which is broadcasted in the United Kingdom, Australia, New Zealand, South Africa, Norway, Iceland, Sweden, Denmark, Finland and the Czech Republic. The discussion about giraffes was in Episode 2 of Series G.

xxi Todd Palmer, Robert Pringle et al

xxii 'Of Ants, Elephants and Acacias: A Tale of Ironic Interdependence' by David Biello, published on 10 January, 2008 at

www.scientificamerican.com

xxiii 'Something Good' by Richard Rodgers and Oscar Hammerstein II and performed by Julie Andrews in *The Sound of Music*

xxiv 'So Long, Farewell', written by Oscar Hammerstein and composed by Richard Rodgers

xxv Sri Bhagavan speaking with Oneness people in Russian speaking countries on 25 October, 2014

xxvi Sri Bhagavan speaking with Oneness people in Latin America, Spain and Turkey on 28 October, 2014

xxvii 'Uptown Funk', written by Mark Ronson, Jeff Bhasker, Bruno Mars and Philip Lawrence and performed by Bruno Mars

xxviii 'I am Australian' written by Bruce Woodley and Dobe Newton and performed by The Seekers

xxix 'The Unexplained Files', series 1, episode 6, aired on the Discovery Channel on 28 September 2014 xxx *Unexplained Files*, series 2, episode 9, on the Discovery Channel on 14 December, 2014.

xxxi 'Devil Inside', written by Andrew Farriss and Michael Hutchence and performed by INXS

xxxii 'No Exit' by Jean-Paul Sartre, published in 1944.

xxxiii 'All I Ask of You', from Andrew Lloyd-Webber's musical Phantom of the Opera, written by Charles Hart and Richard Stilgoe and composed by Andrew Lloyd-Webber.

xxxiv 'Mystify' written by Andrew Farriss and Michael Hutchence and performed by INXS

Made in United States
North Haven, CT
27 May 2024